GET INFORMED, STAY INFORMED

THE OPIOID CRISIS

Natalie Hyde

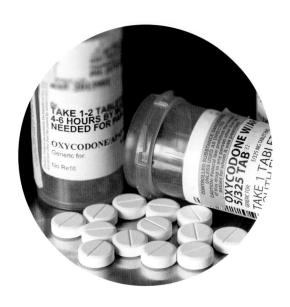

CRABTREE
PUBLISHING COMPANY
WWW.CRABTREEBOOKS.COM

Author: Natalie Hyde
Series research and development:
   Reagan Miller
Editor-in-chief: Lionel Bender
Editor: Ellen Rodger
Proofreaders: Laura Booth,
   Wendy Scavuzzo
Project coordinator: Petrice Custance
Design and photo research: Ben White
Production: Kim Richardson
Print coordinator: Katherine Berti
Consultant: Emily Drew,
   The New York Public Library

Produced for Crabtree
Publishing Company by
Bender Richardson White

Photographs and reproductions:
Alamy
   Bastiaan Slabbers: p. 26–27
   B Christopher: p. 22–23
   Contraband Collection: p. 33
   Gunter Marx: p. 35
   Newscom: p. 30–31
   Richard Levine: p. 10 (bottom)
Getty Images
   Brendan Smialowski: p. 36 (top)
   Chicago Tribune: p. 42–43
   Miami Herald/Walter Michot: p. 16–17
   Miami Herald/C.M. Guerrero: p. 18–19
   Pacific Press/Erik McGregor: p. 24
   Robert Nickelsberg: p. 20–21
   Spencer Platt: p. 14–15, 25, 32 (top)
   Yuri Lashov/AFP: p. 38–39
Shutterstock: box icons, cover, heading band,
   p. 1, 4, 6–7, 8–9, 10 (top), 12, 13, 29, 40–41
   Heidi Besen: p. 37
   Page Light Studios: p. 36 (bottom)
   TopFoto/ImageWorks: p. 34
Diagrams: Stefan Chabluk, using the following as
sources of data: p. 7, 19: www.drugabuse.gov; p. 21:
www.fortune.com, Survey Monkey Poll; p. 26: www.
ama-assn.org; p. 28: www.communityincrisis.org;
p. 32: www.edition.cnn.com, National Forensic Lab.;
p. 39: www.worldatlas.com

Library and Archives Canada Cataloguing in Publication

Hyde, Natalie, 1963-, author
   Opioid crisis / Natalie Hyde.

(Get informed--stay informed)
Includes bibliographical references and index.
Issued in print and electronic formats.
ISBN 978-0-7787-4969-1 (hardcover).--
ISBN 978-0-7787-4973-8 (softcover).--
ISBN 978-1-4271-2122-6 (HTML)

   1. Opioid abuse--Juvenile literature. I. Title.

RC568.O45H93 2018   j362.29'3   C2018-903043-7
                                              C2018-903044-5

Library of Congress Cataloging-in-Publication Data

Names: Hyde, Natalie, 1963- author.
Title: Opioid crisis / Natalie Hyde.
Description: New York : Crabtree Publishing Company, [2019] |
   Series: Get informed--stay informed |
   Includes bibliographical references and index.
Identifiers: LCCN 2018033713 (print) | LCCN 2018035959 (ebook)
   ISBN 9781427121226 (Electronic) |
   ISBN 9780778749691 (hardcover) |
   ISBN 9780778749738 (pbk.)
Subjects: LCSH: Opioid abuse--Juvenile literature. | Drug abuse-
   -Juvenile literature.
Classification: LCC RC568.O45 (ebook) |
   LCC RC568.O45 H93 2019 (print) | DDC 362.29/3--dc23
LC record available at https://lccn.loc.gov/2018033713

Crabtree Publishing Company

www.crabtreebooks.com   1-800-387-7650

Printed in the U.S.A./102018/CG20180810

Published in Canada
Crabtree Publishing
616 Welland Ave.
St. Catharines, ON
L2M 5V6

Published in the United States
Crabtree Publishing
PMB 59051
350 Fifth Avenue, 59th Floor
New York, NY 10118

Published in the United Kingdom
Crabtree Publishing
Maritime House
Basin Road North, Hove
BN41 1WR

Published in Australia
Crabtree Publishing
3 Charles Street
Coburg North
VIC, 3058

CONTENTS

CHAPTER 1   OUR WORLD IN CRISIS   4
What are opioids and what is the nature of the crisis?
How does the crisis affect society? Why is it important
to get informed and to stay informed?

CHAPTER 2   HOW TO GET INFORMED   8
The "Time and Place Rule" and good sources of information.
Key players and different types of source material.
What should you aim for in learning about a new topic?

CHAPTER 3   WHAT IS THE OPIOID CRISIS?   14
The medical use of opioids and how this led to the crisis.
The nature of opioid addiction. Timeline of the crisis.
Attempts to fix the problem.

CHAPTER 4   INFORMATION LITERACY   20
How to sort and evaluate information. Different perspectives
on the subject, including personal stories. The international
status of the opioid crisis.

CHAPTER 5   WHERE THINGS STAND   30
Different strategies for overcoming the crisis, and raising
awareness of the problem and possible solutions.

CHAPTER 6   KEEPING UP TO DATE   40
Guidelines and strategies for staying informed and forming
your own opinion. Recommended sources of information.

GLOSSARY   44
SOURCE NOTES   46
FIND OUT MORE   47
INDEX   48

OUR WORLD IN CRISIS

Opioids are strong pain-reducing drugs. Their overuse causes problems. The opioid crisis has affected every community, class, **ethnic group**, industry, and age group. Misuse of opioids now kills more people in North America each year than breast cancer. In Canada, almost 9 people out of every 100,000 are killed in opioid-related deaths each year and the number is rising. In the United States, the rate is more than 21 people per 100,000.

▶ Opioid use usually starts out as medical treatment for injury and pain, but can lead to drug **addiction** and even **overdose** death.

TAKE 1 TABLET B
MOUTH EVERY
HOURS AS NE
Qty:30 | Refills rec
Store Phone:
Rx #
Prescriber:

QUESTIONS TO ASK

Within this book are three types of boxes with questions to help your critical thinking about the opioid crisis. The icons will help you identify them.

THE CENTRAL ISSUES
Learning about the main points of information.

WHAT'S AT STAKE
Helping you determine how the issue will affect you.

ASK YOUR OWN QUESTIONS
Prompts for gaps in your understanding.

GETTING THE BIG PICTURE

The opioid crisis is so big and widespread that you probably already know people who have been affected: Maybe a neighbor, a friend, or even your own family. You might find yourself wondering why this **epidemic** has happened and why we haven't been able to stop it yet. Maybe you're asking yourself what you could possibly do to help. Before you can answer any of those questions, you need to understand the issue. It's time to get informed.

BEING A RESPONSIBLE CITIZEN

Our world, country, and **community** are constantly changing. Each day there are new problems, dangers, and risks. There are also new solutions, inventions, and ideas. Getting informed about an issue is the first step to being able to talk about it sensibly and in a balanced way, and perhaps bring about change. As a member of **society**, it is your responsibility to be aware of what is happening around you and to discuss and **debate** issues that affect everyone.

INFORMATION IS INVALUABLE

The opioid crisis can touch everyone's lives. You are not safer by not knowing. The expression "Ignorance is bliss" has no truth in the modern world. In fact, the only way to protect yourself from risks in life is to know about them. Knowing and understanding give you the chance to make good decisions and avoid danger. They also allow you to give sensible advice to those who need help.

WHY STAY INFORMED?

Why do you need to stay informed about **current** topics? After all, aren't parents, guardians, teachers, experts, and officials already doing that? Won't they tell you what you need to know? The problem is, what you know affects how you act. By arming yourself with the most current and accurate information, you can make the best decisions based on your unique strengths, weaknesses, fears, and skills. For the opioid crisis, those decisions can mean the difference between life and death.

When others tell you their **interpretation** of facts, details they don't think are important can be left out. Other people might take one side of a debate or another. The points they stress might make the difference in your own understanding of topics or events. If the information you find isn't **accurate** or reliable, you risk walking into danger or being unaware when someone close to you is in trouble.

▲ Smartphones provide us with information, but we still have to determine whether to trust the information.

BUILDING KNOWLEDGE

Don't be afraid to ask questions about a new topic. Find out the **context** of what you want to understand. Context is the setting or surroundings of a topic or event. For instance, the context of the opioid crisis is a time in our history when **chronic** pain is treated with a group of **drugs** called opiates. It is also a time of powerful drug companies. With huge advertising **campaigns**, they can convince the public of the amazing effects of new drugs. They can also hide dangerous **side effects**, such as how addictive a drug may be.

Look for different **perspectives** so you see all sides of the issue. Then, once you have a good understanding, set up ways to stay informed.

THE CENTRAL ISSUES

How did the opioid crisis start, and who does it affect? How might getting informed about it help us to develop strategies for combatting opioid addiction?

DEATHS FROM AN OVERDOSE RELATED TO OPIOIDS PER 100,000 PEOPLE IN THE CANADIAN POPULATION (as at the end of 2017)

- less than 6
- 6 to 9.99
- 10 to 14.99
- more than 15
- no data

DEATHS FROM AN OVERDOSE RELATED TO OPIOIDS PER 100,000 PEOPLE IN THE U.S. POPULATION (as at the end of 2017)

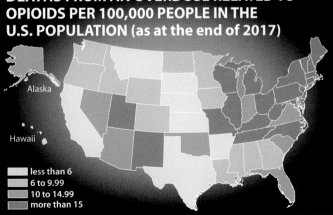

Alaska

Hawaii

- less than 6
- 6 to 9.99
- 10 to 14.99
- more than 15

▲ ▶ Densely populated areas have problems with **trafficking** of opioids. Remote or poorer areas often have fewer opioid treatment centers.

2 HOW TO GET INFORMED

When learning about a new topic, start with getting a good understanding of key background information. The "Time and Place Rule" will help you figure out the best information to learn about your topic. The rule is that information gathered closest to the time and location something happened is probably the most accurate and reliable.

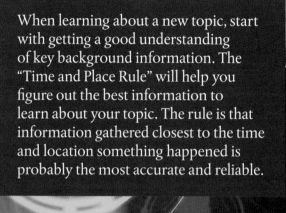

ANALYSIS OF THE SOURSE FILE

|0,085 |0,547 |3,078 |6,0267

▶ Every piece of information should be studied to identify bias and how reliable the source may be.

ID

PRO

6347-E45
25435-Y4457
457497-F9
6244-A79
1287-D8797
363657-C3975

SETTINGS
HISTORY
LOG
DOCUMENTS

NEW SETTINGS

NAME
LAST NAME
CODE
HISTORY
STOCK FACTS

PROFILE
79933-2B
NO PHOTO

MORE

NAME
LAST NAME
PROGRAM
LOCATION
HISTORY
STOCK FACTS

PROFILE
79933-2B
NO PHOTO

MORE

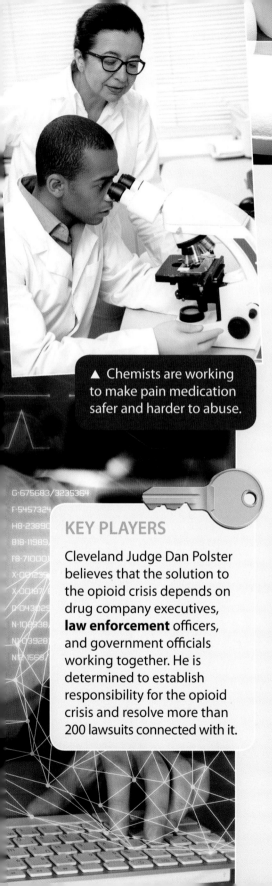

▲ Chemists are working to make pain medication safer and harder to abuse.

KEY PLAYERS

Cleveland Judge Dan Polster believes that the solution to the opioid crisis depends on drug company executives, **law enforcement** officers, and government officials working together. He is determined to establish responsibility for the opioid crisis and resolve more than 200 lawsuits connected with it.

WHERE TO START

For the opioid crisis, examples of good sources from most reliable to less reliable are

- Interviews from users and medics at safe-injection sites that use needle exchanges. These are places supervised by nurses and social workers where drug users can inject drugs
- Reports from doctors and paramedics dealing with opioid-related overdoses
- A study done by a researcher or medical science journalist at an opioid crisis center using interviews with opioid patients
- A government report using evidence collected and prepared by other people.

FOR OR AGAINST

Everyone has their own ideas and opinions about the world. This determines what information is collected and how it is used. Feeling strongly in favor or against something or someone is called **bias.** You should keep in mind that all material contains the creator's bias. Once you identify the bias, you can look behind it to get **objective** information.

With the opioid crisis, those people who blame large drug companies for not warning the public may emphasize false advertising. Those who think that the problem lies with drug dealers might write a report about how criminals are responsible. Those who think society should help with the problem may show how safe-injection sites are lowering overdose numbers.

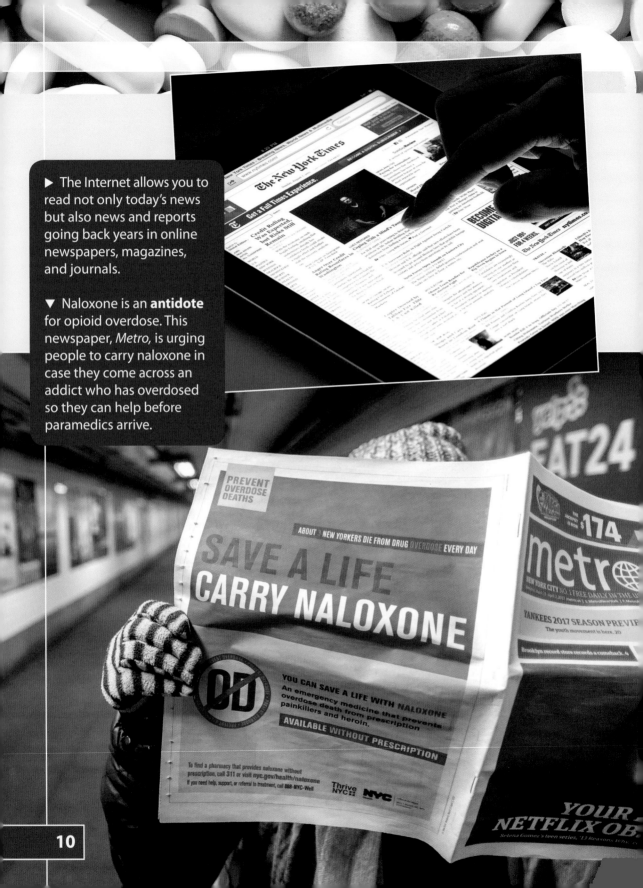

▶ The Internet allows you to read not only today's news but also news and reports going back years in online newspapers, magazines, and journals.

▼ Naloxone is an **antidote** for opioid overdose. This newspaper, *Metro,* is urging people to carry naloxone in case they come across an addict who has overdosed so they can help before paramedics arrive.

WHERE TO FIND INFORMATION

Information is found in source material. Source material is any document, image, audio file, sculpture, or **artifact** connected to a subject. It can be written, visual, or **auditory**. It can be found in museums and libraries; as personal belongings; and, of course, on the Internet. There are three categories of source material—primary, secondary, and tertiary (see sidebar on this page). Primary sources are generally the most reliable and accurate so use these when you can.

The Internet has all types of source material and the information this contains is often more up to date than anything you find in printed form. Some is found on social media websites such as Facebook and Twitter, and in blogs. Other websites, such as online magazines, newspapers, and news programs, give different information. You can also find official government documents and pharmaceutical companies' shareholder reports. This variety of sources can give a broad view of a topic from many different perspectives. Be alert, though, to false Internet information.

WHERE THINGS STAND

So what should you aim for in learning about a new topic? You want to get familiar with what has happened to date. You also want to hear opposite views to balance out any bias. You will benefit from researching both primary and secondary sources. Consider reading or listening to news reports from different stations that are **conservative** and **liberal** in their views. Watch Internet and TV footage where you can get firsthand interviews and visual images. Listen to **podcasts** and read blogs for personal stories. These will help you form a view of a topic.

THE CENTRAL ISSUES

What does it mean to have an "open mind"? What is the value of reading or listening to opinions that are not similar to your own?

SOURCE MATERIALS

Primary sources are the original creators or owners of information, for example, the scientific paper where an opiate was first described, or the pharmaceutical company's medical information provided with the opiate.

Secondary sources are reports, analyses, and interpretations of the primary sources, for example, a hospital's results and observations of people who have used that opiate.

Tertiary sources are summaries or databases of primary and secondary information. They include Wikipedia articles or entries in encyclopedias.

Every topic has its own key players, vocabulary, and ideas. It is important to identify these. Key players are the people or organizations who represent the different sides of the story. In the opioid crisis, judges, doctors, and sometimes the addicts themselves, tell their stories to give us a more rounded picture of the situation.

CLEAR DEFINITIONS

Vocabulary is vital to understanding a topic. If you don't truly know the meaning of words or phrases, you will not be able to express your thoughts clearly. Sometimes we think we know what something means, but we don't. Maybe our understanding comes from what friends have said, or even from what news programs have described. To get accurate information, you should turn to good dictionaries, either in paper or online, for unbiased definitions. For the opioid crisis, you will need to be familiar with the different kinds of drugs, treatments for addiction, and strategies for coping with the crisis.

Key concepts are the central ideas of a topic. Understanding how pain management, addiction, **substance abuse** treatment, drug testing, and government controls work will help you grasp the size, cause, and **scope** of the opioid crisis.

▼ Opium is obtained from the milky fluid that seeps out of poppy pods that have been cut. The fluid dries to a sticky brown substance. Opium contains **morphine,** a strong painkiller that is very addictive. Morphine is used to create other opioids, including heroin, **fentanyl**, and oxycodone.

FACTS AND FIGURES

A good way to learn about and understand a topic is to study graphs, charts, and maps. They can display and interpret facts and figures in novel ways. Just like other source material, graphics can be biased in what information they show or how they show it. A big drug company may want to show how effective its pain medication is, while a concerned doctor may want to show the number of people becoming addicted to prescription drugs for pain.

OPIATES AND OPIOIDS

Opiates are drugs that have their origin in the opium plant. They include opium, morphine, codeine, and heroin. Opioids are chemical compounds used to create drugs in a lab. These include oxycodone, loperamide, oxymorphine, methadone, and fentanyl. The term opioids has come to be used for any substance that effects the brain's opioid receptors. These are the parts of the brain that control pain, feelings of reward, and addiction. All opiates are opioids, but not all opioids are opiates.

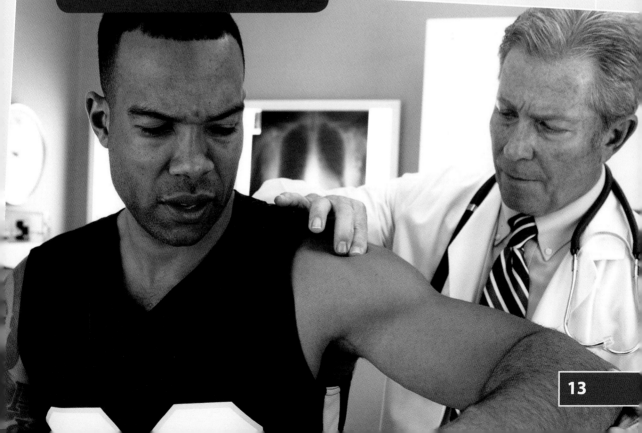

Drugs, drug addiction, and overdoses are not new. So what makes this latest situation so different that it is called a "crisis"? It has to do with how many people are affected, how quickly the numbers are climbing and, so far, a failure to slow down or stop the problem. Today, drug overdoses are the leading cause of death for people under 50 years old. There were more than 64,000 cases in the United States in 2016. Of those drug overdose deaths, more than two-thirds were from opioid drugs. In Canada in 2017, there were 3,987 opioid-related deaths.

▶ A man, suspected of being under the influence of drugs, is stopped and arrested for opioid use by police officers in New York City. Today many police departments are equipping officers with naloxone to reverse the effects of opioid overdose.

Approximately half of all opioid drug overdose deaths are from drugs that were originally prescribed by doctors to relieve serious, long-term pain. This is what has the medical profession, paramedics, teachers, government officials, and parents so worried. In the past, other drug overdose problems were mostly related to illegal, **recreational** drugs such as cocaine.

DEALING WITH THE INCREASE

Doctors, social workers, and lawmakers are scrambling to keep up with the increasing numbers of people becoming addicted to opioids. It is straightforward to regulate illegal drugs. Police can seize shipments of them, stop their production, and arrest drug dealers. Law enforcers face problems in trying to get rid of illegal drugs, but it is easy to recognize what they are and pass laws to control the drug trade.

CONTROLLING ADDICTION

Opioid addiction is much more difficult because not all opiates are illegal. They are useful tools in pain management, work much better than other drugs, and not everyone becomes addicted to them. So it is tricky for laws to be written that will stop abuse of the drugs, but still allow them to be used when needed.

The source of opioids is not always drug dealers and other criminals in back streets and dark alleys, but often doctors and pharmacists. Finding a solution to the opioid crisis has been slow and not very **effective**.

STREET NAMES

If you hear drug dealers or addicts talking, you may not even know they are referring to opioids because they use slang. Some slang terms for opioids are based on the drugs' color, form, and effect, and include: H, hammer, skag, gear, smack, horse, elephant, rock, brown sugar, blue, oxy, nose drops, black tar, China white, white, white dynamite, and dragon.

When the unripe opium poppy seedpod is cut with a blade, a milky sap comes out. When dry, the sap turns brown and sticky. This is opium. In it are **compounds** such as morphine and codeine. They are natural painkillers that are known as opiates. Opiates can be changed in chemical processes to make more drugs. These **synthetic** drugs include oxycodone, methadone, and heroin. Together, the natural and synthetic drugs are called opioids.

THE POWER OF ADDICTION

Opioids are often prescribed after an injury or surgery. They are effective painkillers because they enter the bloodstream, go to the brain, and release **neurotransmitters** that make you feel good or **high**. This creates a rush of happiness and a relief of pain much stronger and more intense than anything that happens naturally, such as by doing something you enjoy. The only way to get that feeling again is to take the drug.

Addiction begins to take hold when the body needs more of the drug to get the same feeling. Next, the body starts to rely on the drug and goes into **withdrawal** if the person stops taking it. Withdrawal symptoms include depression, nausea, muscle cramps, and anxiety. Finally, the body starts craving the drug and the user will do anything to get some. Many people become addicted accidentally. They take prescription drugs to help with pain, but by the time the pain is gone, the opioids have taken hold in the brain. Some abusers fake pain to continue to get legal drugs. Some visit other doctors to get repeat prescriptions. Still others buy opioids from their friends with a prescription. Opioids can also be bought illegally on the street.

WHAT'S AT STAKE?

Why has the use of opioids increased so rapidly in recent years? Why do many addicts avoid getting treatment? Is the crisis beatable?

▶ A U.S. Customs and Border Protection officer stores illegal drugs. It is difficult for law enforcement to seize opioids like they do with other illegal drugs because many have been bought legally in pharmacies.

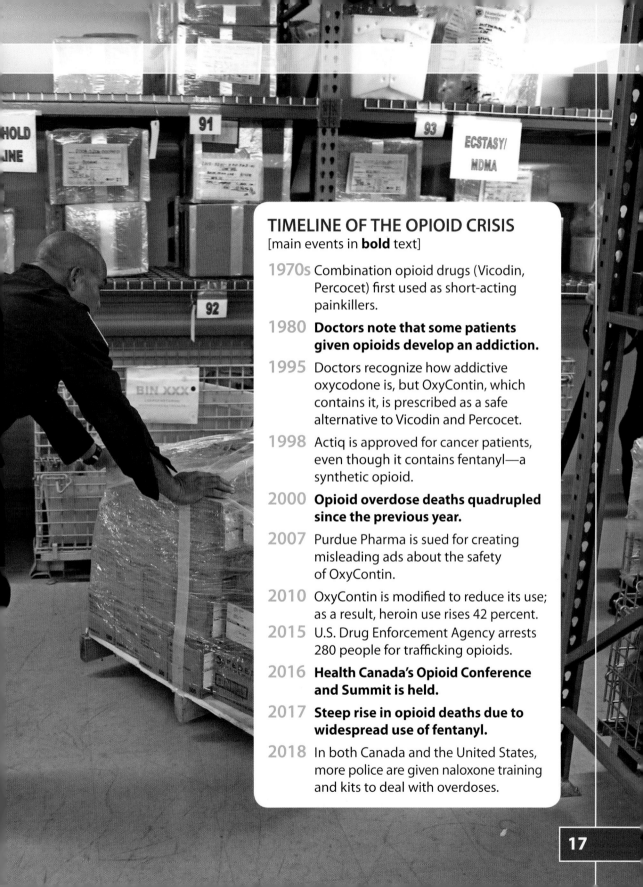

TIMELINE OF THE OPIOID CRISIS
[main events in **bold** text]

1970s Combination opioid drugs (Vicodin, Percocet) first used as short-acting painkillers.

1980 **Doctors note that some patients given opioids develop an addiction.**

1995 Doctors recognize how addictive oxycodone is, but OxyContin, which contains it, is prescribed as a safe alternative to Vicodin and Percocet.

1998 Actiq is approved for cancer patients, even though it contains fentanyl—a synthetic opioid.

2000 **Opioid overdose deaths quadrupled since the previous year.**

2007 Purdue Pharma is sued for creating misleading ads about the safety of OxyContin.

2010 OxyContin is modified to reduce its use; as a result, heroin use rises 42 percent.

2015 U.S. Drug Enforcement Agency arrests 280 people for trafficking opioids.

2016 **Health Canada's Opioid Conference and Summit is held.**

2017 **Steep rise in opioid deaths due to widespread use of fentanyl.**

2018 In both Canada and the United States, more police are given naloxone training and kits to deal with overdoses.

For the thousands of years opium and opiates have been around and used to ease pain and promote sleep, there have been problems with users becoming addicted to them. In the last century, many more powerful versions of the drugs were produced. Opioids became even more popular with doctors trying to manage their patients' pain.

Oxycodone is a **synthesized** opioid that was developed in Germany in 1916. OxyContin is a slow-release type of oxycodone. It was approved in the United States in 1995. The maker, Purdue Pharma, launched a large marketing campaign to doctors and medical school students. It claimed the drug was safer than other opioids with none of the dangerous side effects, including addiction. OxyContin prescriptions soared—and so did addiction to it.

> " In its lawsuit settlement, Purdue Pharma acknowledged that it had *"fraudulently and misleadingly marketed OxyContin as less addictive, less subject to abuse, and less likely to cause withdrawal symptoms than other pain medications."* "

TRYING TO FIX THE PROBLEM

It wasn't until 2007 that the truth about the dangers of OxyContin became widely known. The numbers of people addicted and abusing opioids were staggering. Some addicts were snorting the drug. Others were crushing it and injecting it into their bloodstream. Because of this, Purdue pulled the drug from the market. It replaced it with OxyNeo, a pill that couldn't be crushed. But the drug was still just as addictive.

With this information, prescriptions for oxycodone fell. But other opioids were taken instead. The addiction was still there. **Banning** a certain prescription drug is not the answer since many people depend on it medically. Several steps have been taken to solve the issue. Medical schools are tackling misinformation with new courses on opioids and their dangers. New guidelines are being created to advise doctors to try other methods of pain control before turning to opioids. If opioids are needed for pain, they urge doctors to prescribe only low doses for short periods of time.

OVERDOSE DEATHS INVOLVING OPIOIDS, BY TYPE OF OPIOID, UNITED STATES, 2000 – 2016

Deaths per 100,000 population

Legend:
- Any Opioid
- Other Synthetic Opioids
- Heroin
- Natural & Semi-Synthetic Opioids
- Methadone

Y-axis: 0, 1, 2, 3, 4, 5, 6, 7, 8, 9, 10, 11, 12, 13, 14

X-axis: 2000, 2001, 2002, 2003, 2004, 2005, 2006, 2007, 2008, 2009, 2010, 2011, 2012, 2013, 2014, 2015, 2016

◀ Paramedics attend an overdosed opioid user. The Center for Disease Control in the United States reports that opioids are a factor in two out of three accidental overdose deaths.

To get informed about a topic, you need to study a range of relevant source materials and sort and **evaluate** the information they contain. Learning how to do this is known as information literacy. For the opioid crisis, determining who is to blame or what went wrong can have different answers, depending on who you talk to or what you read. For example, a U.S. public poll taken in 2017 showed that most people thought doctors and those hooked on opioids were to blame (see graphic opposite). Drug companies were much more responsible.

> " These [addicts] are not stupid people. They know they can't do this much longer. Think of the power of that addiction. "
>
> Dr. Jeffrey Turnbull, internal medicine specialist

▼ Crisis service centers provide overdose rescue kits to the community, needle exchange programs, and counseling for vulnerable people in order to combat the epidemic.

A BALANCED VIEW

Everyone has a bias, and what someone tells you will reflect what he or she believes. Knowing this, the first step to getting a balanced view is to identify the different sides of the story. In the opioid crisis, there are many perspectives. Doctors need ways to help their patients control pain. Nurses and paramedics deal with overdose victims. Drug companies try to develop new medicines that are more effective and safer. Law enforcement officers deal with criminal behavior such as drug dealing. Politicians are supposed to work for the people who voted for them by drafting new laws to make society safer.

Once you identify the main sides, consider each viewpoint and look for bias that might slant articles, images, and interviews. Politicians want to be reelected; companies need to make money to stay afloat; doctors take an oath to help patients; and paramedics try to save lives. Families, employers, society, and the addicts themselves are also affected by the opioid crisis.

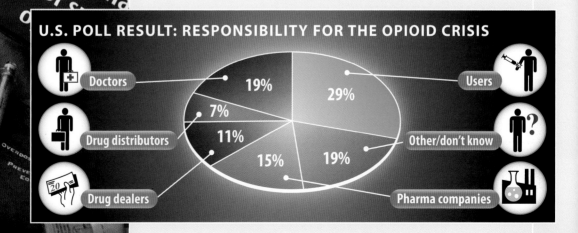

U.S. POLL RESULT: RESPONSIBILITY FOR THE OPIOID CRISIS

- Doctors — 19%
- Drug distributors — 7%
- Drug dealers — 11%
- Users — 29%
- Other/don't know — 15%
- Pharma companies — 19%

When we look at drug addiction and overdose deaths from the point of view of families, we can see the **profound** effect they have. A spouse or partner who is an addict puts a huge strain on the relationship. His or her need for money for drugs can drain finances. When savings run out, the person might turn to criminal behavior to get money or drugs. Cravings and withdrawal can lead to anger, violence, or depression. Relationships may have a difficult time surviving a drug addiction.

PUTTING A STRAIN ON CHILDREN

The National Institute on Drug Abuse says an estimated 25 percent of American children grow up in homes where there is substance abuse. These children are more at risk for anxiety and depression—as well as violence in the home. When the addict is a parent, children sometimes take on the role of caregiver, looking after the parent and younger siblings. Seeing a parent engage in risky behavior to pay for their addiction can be confusing. Children may not know what to do about their feelings of fear, guilt, and anger.

PERSONAL STORIES

Information from families about the opioid crisis is often in the form of personal stories, diaries, blogs, or interviews. The details can include a lot of emotion and anger. This type of information might deal with assigning blame. Individuals want to know who is responsible for the tragedy in their life. These stories are a good way to round out research. They can give facts and figures, faces and names. These stories might let you see yourself in the same situation and feel **empathy** for addicts and overdose victims.

KEY PLAYERS

Dr. Jeffrey Turnbull is an internal medicine specialist who works with the Ottawa Inner City Health organization and spends much of his time on the streets helping opioid addicts. Dr. Turnbull believes that solving problems like poverty and homelessness can help prevent people from turning to drugs.

▶ These protestors in Washington, D.C., are trying to raise awareness of the opioid crisis and prod their government into action.

WHAT'S AT STAKE?

LOW RISK — HIGH RISK

If more resources are not directed at families struggling with the opioid crisis, what could be the long-term effects for families or children? Do you think the effects can pass from generation to generation?

Children Over Wealth
In Loving Memory
Ryan Medeiros-Tavares
4-1-90 – 9-11-13
STOP KILLING OUR
Children for Your Financial Benefit

Drug
over
doses
now
Kill
more
than
car
crashes

Big Pharma
is
America's
WMD!

MY
SON
HELP ME
Save
Yours
Joshua
Graves

KERRI
~Princess~

GONE TOO SOON—
L♥VED FOREVER!

FDA NEEDS NEW
LEADERSHIP!

FED UP
FOR MY
BEST
FRIEND!

PAINKILLERS KILL MORE
THAN PAIN!

R.I.P. Princess Kerri

WITH
LOSING
FRIENDS

Sistah

> *It's just so stigmatized, and I can't bear to think that there are families today that have family members where they know that there is addiction at play but are too ashamed to talk about it.*
>
> Andrey Ostrovsky, former Medicaid chief medical officer

23

If you run a business, you need to have **dependable,** honest employees. About 75 percent of chronic substance abusers work part or full time. Statistics show that workers who are high on drugs are more likely to cause injury or damage. Driving while high is just as dangerous as driving drunk. Workers who use heavy machinery can cause serious accidents for themselves and others. The cost of substance abuse is huge for the economy.

Substance abusers also tend to be **unreliable.** They are more likely to arrive late or miss days at work. Even on the job, they frequently make mistakes. A report by the U.S. Drug Enforcement Administration shows that people with substance abuse problems often have conflicts with coworkers. If users cannot keep up with their jobs, others have to take on a larger share of the workload. This makes staff angry and costs a company in lost time and money.

▼ City officials, African American and Latinx Community leaders, doctors, counselors, and civil rights activists protest on the steps on New York's City Hall to demand government action in the opioid crisis.

> *A drug-free workplace is an important goal, and it's something you need to fight for in your EAP (Employee Assistance Programs).*
>
> Barry McCaffrey, retired U.S. Army General

WHAT'S AT STAKE

How does the opioid crisis affect the economy? Why is any action plan against this crisis expensive? Who should pay for the **rehabilitation** programs?

SIGNS AND SIGNALS

The effects of the opioid crisis are often worse for small businesses. They also have a harder time paying higher rates for insurance. They don't have the money to pay for programs for drug-free workplaces. Any companies that do work for the U.S. government have to follow the Drug-Free Workplace Act of 1988. That includes drug testing and penalties for people who use drugs while at work.

It is sometimes difficult for employers to identify workers who have an opioid addiction. Some may fall asleep on the job, but others still manage to do their tasks. Employers look at workers for signs such as:

- changes in their moods
- not keeping clean
- taking a longer time than usual for tasks
- making poor decisions
- not showing up for appointments or missing deadlines
- becoming confused or forgetting things.

A PERSONAL STORY

Dan Baker began taking opioids with a prescription from his doctor for a sports injury. He began relying on the drugs to get through the day. Then he started doctor shopping—visiting several doctors to get multiple prescriptions for pills. He sought help for drug addiction but turned to heroin to "feel normal." Out of medical treatment, he lost his job and spiraled down again. He went back into treatment but got kicked out for using drugs to help with the cravings. Wanting just one more party, he used some "bad" drugs and died of an overdose. He was 25.

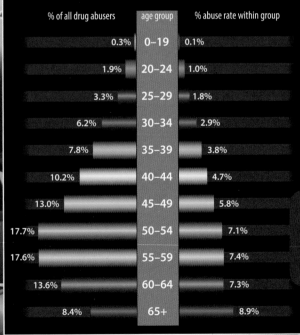

OPIOID ABUSE IN U.S.A. AMONG PEOPLE OF DIFFERENT AGE GROUPS

% of all drug abusers	age group	% abuse rate within group
0.3%	0–19	0.1%
1.9%	20–24	1.0%
3.3%	25–29	1.8%
6.2%	30–34	2.9%
7.8%	35–39	3.8%
10.2%	40–44	4.7%
13.0%	45–49	5.8%
17.7%	50–54	7.1%
17.6%	55–59	7.4%
13.6%	60–64	7.3%
8.4%	65+	8.9%

◀ Opioid addiction can affect any age group. People over 50 are at a high risk for misusing their prescriptions.

Even though addiction is a personal event, its effects are felt all through society. The violence and crime that spring from addicts' demands might affect you or your family.

Some families see more child abuse and violence in the home. Police, teachers, counselors, and health care workers have to work harder to help the victims.

Reports show that about 18 percent of prison **inmates** have committed crimes to get money for drugs. The crimes include robbery and burglary in homes and offices, and mugging people in streets and parks and on public transportation. Stores lose product because of shoplifting. Cars are stolen. The deeper the addiction, the more serious the crimes committed to get money to buy drugs. With the opioid crisis at such a high level, the number of thefts is especially high. That costs everyone money in insurance and in taxes to pay for police and court services to deal with the higher crime rate. Statistics show that more than $500 billion are lost each year in the United States alone in dealing with the opioid crisis.

ADDICTION DEMOGRAPHICS

Prescription abuse rates increase with age. They can also fluctuate geographically. One area of the country may have more abuse among people over 35 who became addicted after a work injury. Another may have more young people who abuse opioids. Young adults abuse prescription drugs for a number of reasons. Some do it to get high or relieve emotional pain. Older people are also at risk. When prescribed painkillers, they may take the wrong **dosage**, or mix prescription drugs with alcohol.

Prescription abuse leads to addiction, and addiction too often leads to overdose deaths. Overdose deaths are highest among 25 to 34 year olds and seniors. Each year, the number rises. Now, in Canada, about 10 people die of drug overdose per day. In the United States, that number is 115 people per day.

◄ Education is the first step in reducing opioid abuse and the number of overdose deaths.

No one plans to ruin their life being an addict. But scientists have found that some people are more likely than others to become addicted to drugs. These people are born with **genes** that make them naturally susceptible to becoming addicted. People with mental illness are also at risk. Statistics show that if you are dealing with emotional pain or have friends who abuse drugs, you are more likely to abuse them yourself. People who have suffered from physical or sexual abuse might also turn to drugs to ease their situation.

Some people in society think that addicts are just bad people who have no willpower. They think if habitual drug users really wanted to, they could just say no and stop. But drugs, and especially opioids, change a person's brain. When a person does things he or she enjoys, such as eat their favorite food or meet friends, their brain normally releases feel-good chemicals. Opioids prompt the brain to flood the body with these chemicals. With addiction, only the drugs make the addict feel good.

KICKING THE HABIT

An addict's life is ruled by their addiction. When you look at what their world has become, you see health problems, money problems, and loneliness.

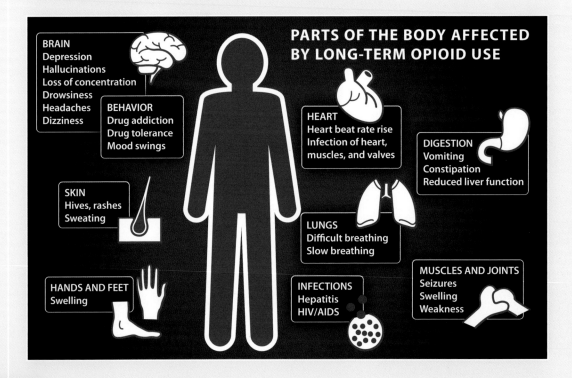

PARTS OF THE BODY AFFECTED BY LONG-TERM OPIOID USE

BRAIN
Depression
Hallucinations
Loss of concentration
Drowsiness
Headaches
Dizziness

BEHAVIOR
Drug addiction
Drug tolerance
Mood swings

HEART
Heart beat rate rise
Infection of heart, muscles, and valves

DIGESTION
Vomiting
Constipation
Reduced liver function

SKIN
Hives, rashes
Sweating

LUNGS
Difficult breathing
Slow breathing

HANDS AND FEET
Swelling

INFECTIONS
Hepatitis
HIV/AIDS

MUSCLES AND JOINTS
Seizures
Swelling
Weakness

When a person spends all their time finding drugs, getting money to buy drugs, and using drugs, there isn't much time for them to do anything else. Addicts often lose their jobs, friends, and families. Also, as their addiction to opioids increases, so does their chance of dying due to overdose.

Personal stories from addicts are powerful. They give a perspective on how and why addiction happens. These stories can open your eyes to how a life can spiral downward. They can also help you understand just how difficult it is to kick the habit. Many addicts begin drug rehabilitation programs. With their brain and body telling them how much they need opioids, they often fail several times before they manage to get clean. Each time they fail, they run the risk of overdosing.

ASK YOUR OWN QUESTIONS

Is treatment and recovery from opioid addiction similar to other addictions such as alcoholism or gambling? Do these factors make it a more difficult addiction to treat?

PERSONAL STORY

American citizen Alicia Campbell was arrested in October 2014 for possession of heroin. She was sent to a rehabilitation program for heroin and opioid addiction. She began writing in a journal while in drug rehab. She wrote that she wanted to go back to her home in Missouri and go back to school. She was released from rehab in March 2016. But the pull of the addiction was so strong, that she began using again. She died of a heroin overdose less than a week after being released.

◀ Medications and talk therapy can help with depression and other mental illnesses that can make a person more at risk of drug addiction.

WHERE THINGS STAND

When you study a historical event, you can learn about all its causes and outcomes. Information about the event has often been collected and sorted and is easy to find. Experts and scientists have published their findings, and historians, authors, and reporters have interpreted them. An issue that is ongoing is a different story. With current events, factors are always changing. Information comes from many sources with different perspectives. It is sometimes hard to determine who all the key players are.

▼ On October 26, 2017, Donald Trump, president of the United States, declared the opioid crisis a national health emergency under the Public Health Services Act. Funding for the crisis was approved by Congress and more funding is planned for 2018 and 2019.

WHAT'S AT STAKE?

Why is it vital to have accurate information? Who might gain from spreading false information?

CHECK IT OUT

As an event progresses, information is created. In the action, or "heat of the moment," information may not be recorded accurately or is misinterpreted. False information often doesn't get corrected and it spreads. To establish the truth, you need to look for accurate information. For the opioid crisis, the following are key and reliable sources of information. More are listed on pages 46-47.

- government health organizations such as Health Canada and the U.S. Department of Health and Human Resources
- independent health organizations such as the Canadian Institute for Health Information or WHO (World Health Organization)
- medical information leaflets given with any drug or that you may find at your local pharmacy or doctor's office
- research papers on opioid addiction, for example, those found in medical journals such as *The Lancet*
- drug-user group reports and blogs such as Nora's blog on the National Institute on Drug Abuse's website (www.drugabuse.gov/about-nida/noras-blog)
- quality national newspapers and magazines, for example, *The New York Times, The Washington Post, USA Today, The Globe and Mail, TIME,* and *The Economist*
- TV documentaries such as PBS's *Understanding the Opioid Epidemic.*
- TV news on CNN and the BBC.

In the fight to contain the opioid crisis, society is losing the battle. Opioid-related overdose deaths are still rising in the United States and Canada. Even though new prescriptions for opioid drugs are falling, the crisis is still worsening. As doctors cut back on dosages, people are turning to synthetic street drugs to manage their pain.

IN THE UNITED STATES

In the United States, the government is planning on a large media campaign to make more people aware of the dangers of opioid addiction. It is also trying to make borders stronger and harder for criminals to smuggle in illegal drugs. The United States is also making naloxone more available. It is increasing funding to treatment centers, especially for veterans. The funding will also help create a national overdose tracking system similar to those used by some states. This will allow for quicker response for hard-hit areas.

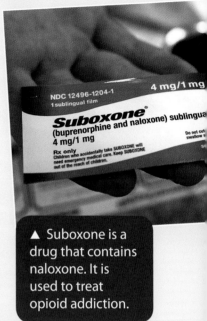

▲ Suboxone is a drug that contains naloxone. It is used to treat opioid addiction.

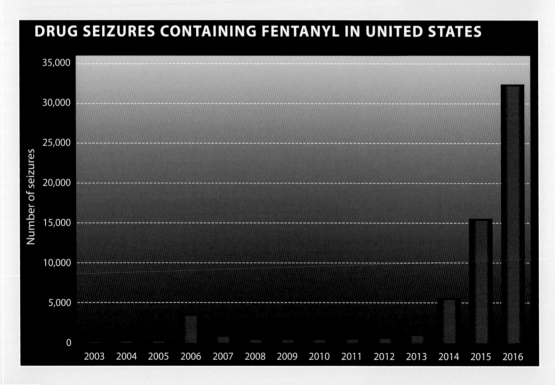

DRUG SEIZURES CONTAINING FENTANYL IN UNITED STATES

Number of seizures

35,000 — 30,000 — 25,000 — 20,000 — 15,000 — 10,000 — 5,000 — 0

2003 2004 2005 2006 2007 2008 2009 2010 2011 2012 2013 2014 2015 2016

IN CANADA

The Canadian government is planning to fight the crisis in four ways—preventing misuse; reducing the harm caused by addiction; better treatments for addicts; and enforcing the laws. Cities across the country are reporting successful strategies and are using public alerts when they suspect drugs **tainted** with fentanyl are in the area. Most provinces in Canada have passed Good Samaritan laws. These laws protect people who telephone 911 when they see a person who has overdosed so they won't be arrested themselves even if they have drugs on them at the scene.

Naloxone is a drug that reverses the effects of opioids. It can save lives. In several Canadian cities, police, paramedics, and firefighters carry it, but also public library staff and some citizens are trained to use it. Cities make it freely available for anyone who admits a history of opioid use or people who may help stop an overdose. Naloxone saves lives.

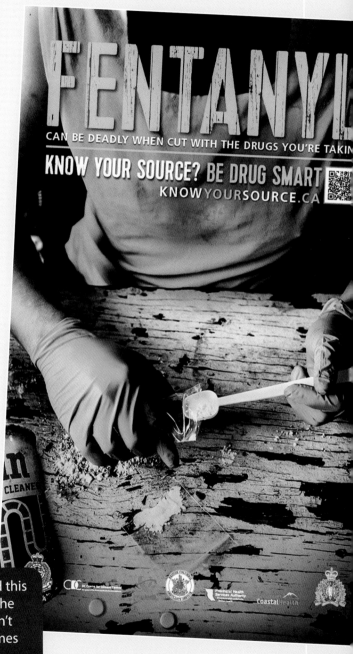

▶ The Canadian government created this poster in 2016 to raise awareness of the dangers of fentanyl. Opioid users aren't always aware that fentanyl is sometimes cut into other drugs they are taking.

Sometimes false information is spread so widely or repeated so often that people think it's true. These **myths** can cloud the issue and make it difficult to make good decisions about your behavior. The opioid crisis creates a lot of fear, so it is important to check facts. Some of the myths about the crisis are:

Opioids are the best medicine for pain relief.
That often depends on the nature of the pain. The American Medical Association published a study on opioid pain relievers. They found that over a year of taking them, opioids were not noticeably better than other pain medication for back pain or arthritis. Sports injuries treated with physical therapy, anti-inflammatory drugs, and **acupuncture** often repair and heal well. However, the pain associated with cancer and other life-threatening diseases is often treated with opioid drugs. The risk of addiction is not considered as important as keeping these patients comfortable.

Addiction only happens to those who are already addicts.
Studies of heroin addicts show that four out of five of them started their addiction with prescription opioids—not the other way around. Most opioid addicts turn to heroin because it is cheaper than prescription opioids, widespread, and easier to get.

Banning opioids will fix the problem.
Prohibition made alcohol illegal. It was still made and sold, but the alcohol market just went underground. Stopping drugs from being smuggled in and sold on the streets is a difficult battle. Heroin and fentanyl are already banned, but their use is still on the rise. Banning opioids will not stop their misuse and addiction.

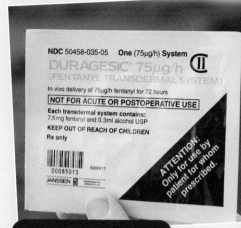

▲ Duragesic is a pain patch that delivers fentanyl slowly. Dozens of overdoses and deaths linked to the patch led the U.S. Federal Drug Administration to pull it from the market.

ASK YOUR OWN QUESTIONS

Why do people hang on to misinformation even after it has been debunked? Why is it harder to remove misinformation in the digital age than it was before the Internet?

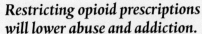

Restricting opioid prescriptions will lower abuse and addiction.

Since 2011, the number of prescriptions for opioid drugs has fallen, but the number of addictions and overdose deaths keeps increasing. Studies show that is because heroin and fentanyl are the main factors in rising numbers. Fentanyl is showing up in more and more illegal drugs, often without users knowing it is in there.

▼ The use of cannabis (marijuana) is legal in Canada and in some states in the United States. Studies are showing that patients report cannabis is just as good as opioids for pain relief, while reducing the chance of addiction or overdose.

"Opioids are an important class of medication for easing suffering at the end of life and when prescribed short-term for severe acute pain. But when opioids are prescribed long-term for chronic pain, we may actually be harming far more patients than we're helping."

Dr. Andrew Kolodny, Chief Medical Officer at Phoenix House Foundation

Fighting back the opioid tide in West Virginia

33 photos taken by Brendan SMIALOWSKI from 19 April to 20 April 2017.

Pictures available on www.afpforum.com: US-health-drugs-WestVirginia

www.afp.com

▲ This photo essay is by Brendan Smialowski. He captured images of daily life in a community affected by the opioid crisis to tell the story of how devastating the crisis is.

▼ A group of medical students in Boston is asking that Safe-injection Sites be set up in their city. They believe SISs will save lives and prevent injuries from dirty needles thrown away outside, such as here in Paul Revere Park.

Some strategies to fight the opioid crisis are working. This is because more information is being discovered on how opioids affect the brain and other body organs and how to treat addiction. New drugs are being created that might some day replace opioids.

Safe-injection Sites (SISs) are a hot topic. They are places where people can use drugs, whether they are legal or not. Staff are there to give out clean needles and **dispose** of used ones. They also carry naloxone in case of accidental overdose. People who support these spaces say they protect the public. Clean needles mean fewer cases of spreading serious diseases such as AIDS and **hepatitis.** Dirty needles are not thrown out into the community where they might harm children, pets, or adults. Staff members are able to prevent overdose deaths by giving life-saving drugs quickly.

People against SISs say they encourage individuals to use drugs. They do not want society helping drug users continue to use instead of getting them into rehabilitation. They also are worried an SIS will attract substance abusers from other areas into their community.

NEW INITIATIVES

Other changing ideas include new rules to help patients dispose of leftover prescription drugs so they don't get into the wrong hands. New training is being developed for first responders to identify opioid overdose and treat with naloxone. More money may be directed to the creation of new types of pain medications. Funds might also be used for services for children and youth affected by the crisis. To find out more, look for studies published by health organizations.

▼ This protester holds up his sign as President Trump visits Manchester, New Hampshire. Many people think opioids are still popular because big drug companies are making lots of money off them.

ASK YOUR OWN QUESTIONS

Is there anything individuals can do to prevent the crisis from getting worse? Where is your nearest safe-injection site, and how can you combat the crisis in your neighborhood?

Around the world, there are huge differences in opioid-related death numbers. Germany had only 1,333 opioid-related deaths in 2016 even though it prescribes opioids almost as much as the United States. And its numbers are not soaring. Officials at the German Center for Addiction Issues say there are two reasons. First, the rules are much stricter for doctors prescribing opioids. They give the drugs for severe pain from cancer but not for chronic pain such as back pain. Second, the doctors are trained to look for early signs of addiction. They recognize when patients are in danger of becoming addicted and quickly work to **wean** them off the drugs.

Other countries have had some success in reversing the number of drug-related deaths, including opioids. Italy, Australia, Luxembourg, Greece, and Switzerland have all tackled the problem by providing methadone to help users overcome their opioid addiction. Countries such as Sweden, the United Kingdom, and Finland have strict rules and restrictions for addicts to get methadone. They have not been as successful in slowing the number of opioid-related deaths.

A DIFFERENT TYPE OF CRISIS

Several other countries have a different opioid crisis: They have little to no access to the drugs. While misuse of opioids can lead to addiction and overdose deaths, no opioids is a problem for cancer patients who are near the end of their life and for people suffering the pain of severe burns. In Africa, Latin America, and part of Asia, people have to put up with horrible pain that morphine could ease. A shortage of doctors to prescribe the medicine and complex licenses mean patients in many poorer countries go without opioids.

▼ Russian federal drug officers burn bags of methadone, which is illegal in Russia. Their method of treating addiction is for addicts to quit **"cold turkey"** and suffer the withdrawal symptoms.

" There is a lack of awareness of the drugs people are using, meaning they can't protect themselves. "

Christopher Jones, U.S. Department of Health

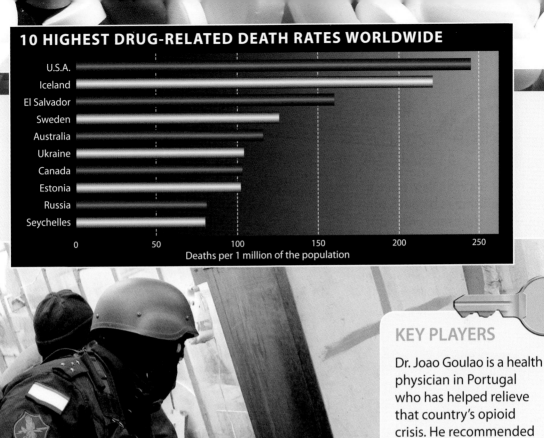

10 HIGHEST DRUG-RELATED DEATH RATES WORLDWIDE

Country	Deaths per 1 million of the population
U.S.A.	
Iceland	
El Salvador	
Sweden	
Australia	
Ukraine	
Canada	
Estonia	
Russia	
Seychelles	

Deaths per 1 million of the population

KEY PLAYERS

Dr. Joao Goulao is a health physician in Portugal who has helped relieve that country's opioid crisis. He recommended decriminalization of drug use. He also put the focus on treatment, rehabilitation, and harm reduction. Harm reduction refers to finding ways to reduce the chance of substance abusers harming themselves or others when they can't or won't stop using drugs. One example is needle exchange programs.

6 KEEPING UP TO DATE

Getting up to date on a topic or issue, such as the opioid crisis, is the first step to staying informed and playing your part in society. It helps you establish the key information, major players, and where to look for the latest and best news. If you fail to do this, you can't make the best decisions for yourself.

▶ It's not enough to just find and read articles on the Internet. You have to check for context, bias, and the source of the material.

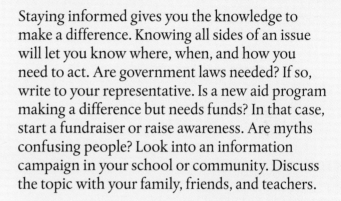

INTERNET SEARCHES

When looking at websites, address extensions can help identify the sources of the information.

.gov (government)— official government organizations or departments. You may not be able to access all areas of these websites.

.org (organization)— usually nonprofit organizations and charities. You may have to register to use these.

.com (commercial)— mostly businesses. It is the most widely used web address extension.

Country extensions:

.ca	Canada
.us	United States
.au	Australia
.uk	United Kingdom
.ru	Russia
.de	Germany

Staying informed gives you the knowledge to make a difference. Knowing all sides of an issue will let you know where, when, and how you need to act. Are government laws needed? If so, write to your representative. Is a new aid program making a difference but needs funds? In that case, start a fundraiser or raise awareness. Are myths confusing people? Look into an information campaign in your school or community. Discuss the topic with your family, friends, and teachers.

CHECK SOURCES AND CREDENTIALS

As you keep up to date, be on the lookout for bias and fake news. Your **news diet** will come with opinions and arguments. Try to stay objective when you are researching, and gather all information before you form your own viewpoint. Don't be afraid to ask questions when you don't understand something.

Try to use primary sources whenever you can, and remember to check the sources of your information. Organizations that sell goods or services will always promote the viewpoint that keeps them profitable.

Check credentials. Lots of people call themselves doctors, scientists, or experts. See where they went to school, what organization they work for, or what experience they have. Double-check facts and figures. Use multiple sources to see if they all say the same thing. If the numbers or facts are different, dig deeper to understand why. Keep your eyes and ears open for the latest news on the topic.

Printed newspapers, magazines, and books in libraries are great sources of information. They can give you excellent backgrounds to a topic but, by the nature of their production, they are not very up to date. Television, radio, and the Internet offer much more current news, facts, and figures, and give you access to information from around the world, often constantly and instantly. The ability to see multiple points of view and international research helps give you a better overall picture of an issue.

Adding international news and scientific studies on your topic is an important part of your news diet. Other countries and cultures can view an issue in a very different light. They might have had success in solving social problems in a new way. They may have failed to improve a problem. Both situations are very helpful in your own understanding. They can lead you to a new way of thinking about a topic and what can be done to prevent a crisis.

ON ALERT

On the Internet, alerts set up with search engines are a quick and easy way to try to make sure you don't miss news from anywhere in the world. Search online to find instructions on how to set this up. Starting your own news feed on a topic is also possible. Search for "news services" online. Newsreader sites let you customize your news feed.

There are also several apps you can use on your smartphone to browse online newspapers, blogs, podcasts, and magazines. Examples of these include Flipboard, Feedly, and Google Currents. The more news services you use, the wider your breadth of knowledge will become.

ASK YOUR OWN QUESTIONS

What would you do if your doctor prescribed an opioid for a sports injury—for yourself or for a friend?

SEARCH TIPS

In search windows on the Internet:

• Use quotation marks around a phrase to find that exact combination of words (for example, "fentanyl overdose").

• Use the minus sign to eliminate certain words from your search (for example, Opioid crisis -heroin).

• Use a colon and an extension to search a specific site (for example, OxyContin:.gov for all government website mentions of the drug).

• Use the word Define and a colon to search for word definitions (for example, Define: opioid).

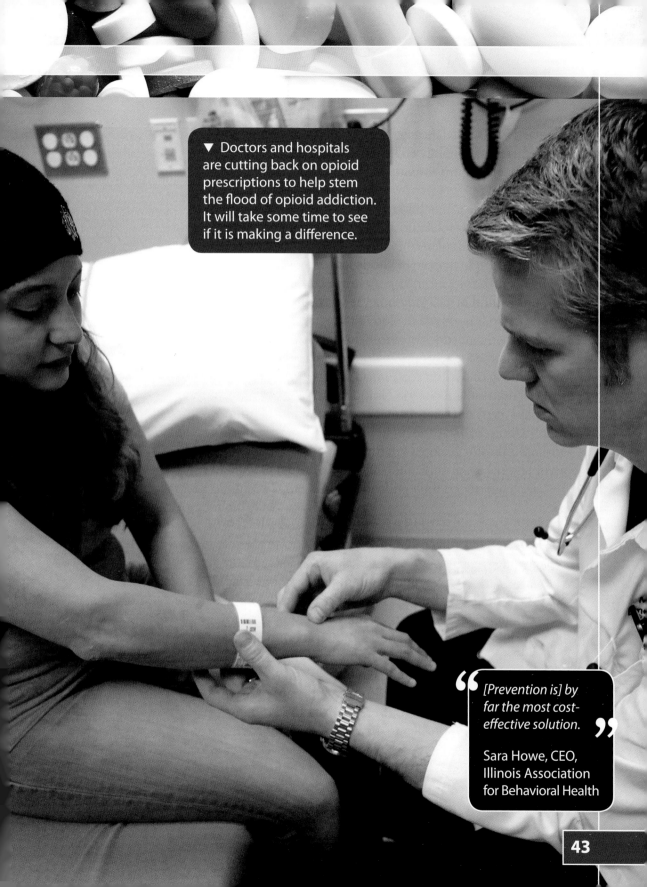

▼ Doctors and hospitals are cutting back on opioid prescriptions to help stem the flood of opioid addiction. It will take some time to see if it is making a difference.

"[Prevention is] by far the most cost-effective solution."

Sara Howe, CEO, Illinois Association for Behavioral Health

GLOSSARY

accurate Correct in all details

acupuncture A body treatment that inserts needles into the skin to ease pain

addiction The habit or condition of wanting something repeatedly

antidote Something that overcomes a poison or ill feeling

artifact An object or item made by someone

auditory Relating to the sense of hearing

banning Not allowing

bias Prejudice in favor for or against something or someone

campaigns Plans with a goal or objective

chronic Long-term, usually related to an illness or pain

cold turkey Suddenly stopping taking a drug; often causes terrible symptoms

community People living together as a group or in a neighborhood

compounds Things made up of two or more elements

conservative Cautious or slow to change

context The circumstances or situation surrounding something

current Happening now

debate Discussion between the key players

dependable Trustworthy

dispose Get rid of

dosage The amount of medicine to be used

drugs Medicines

effective Successful in getting a result

empathy The ability to share the feelings of others

epidemic A big outbreak of a disease in a community

ethnic group People with the same cultural background

evaluate Work out the importance or worth

fentanyl A synthetic opioid

genes Contents of cells that determine characteristics making each person unique

hepatitis A serious disease of the liver

high Feeling good, especially from the effect of drugs

inmates People in prison

interpretation An explanation or meaning of something

law enforcement The people who uphold the law such as police

liberal Free-thinking; with limited power of the government

morphine A strong drug made from opium to ease pain

myths Traditional or widely held belief that cannot be verified

neurotransmitters Chemicals in the brain that help nerve signals transfer

news diet The sources you use to get your news

objective Without bias; a balanced viewpoint

overdose Too much of a drug

perspectives Viewpoints, outlooks

podcasts Spoken information made available on the Internet

profound Deep, meaningful

recreational For fun or enjoyment rather than medical need

rehabilitation To bring someone back to health

scope The breadth or extent of subject matter

side effects Other reactions to a drug not related to the treatment

society People living and working together in a country in an ordered way

substance abuse Using too much of a drug or using it too often

synthesized Made artificially by combining chemicals

synthetic Made from human-made materials

tainted Polluted with something

trafficking Dealing or trading in something illegally

unreliable Cannot depend on it

wean Slowly get used to doing without something

withdrawal Unpleasant symptoms, usually when stopping the use of drugs

SOURCE NOTES

QUOTATIONS

p 18: Maclean's: "Inside the history of Canada's opioid crisis." www.macleans.ca

p 20: Maclean's: "Facing the opioid crisis, an establishment doctor heads to the streets." www.macleans.ca

p 23: NPR: "Understanding the Struggle Against Opioid Addiction." www.npr.org

p 25: Society for Human Resource Management: "Former Drug Czar: Drugs in the Workplace and Understated Crisis." www.shrm.org

p 27: *Psychology Today*: "The Solution to the Opioid Crisis." www.psychologytoday.com

p 35: USC Annenberg, Center for Health Journalism: "Busting Pain Medicine Myths with Andrew Kolodny." www.centerforhealthjournalism.org

p 38: Reuters: "U.S. opioid crisis could spread to Europe, experts say." www.reuters.com

p 43: *Time Health*: "Here's what it would cost to fix the opioid crisis, according to 5 Experts." http://time.com

REFERENCES USED FOR THIS BOOK

Chapter 1: Our World in Crisis, pp. 4–7
• Government of Canada, "National Report: Apparent Opioid-related Deaths." www.canada.ca
• Centers for Disease Control and Prevention, "Drug Overdose Death Data." www.cdc.gov
• Kounan, Nadia. CNN. www.cnn.com

Chapter 2: How to Get Informed, pp. 8–13
• Feeley, Jef and Hopkins, Jared. Bloomberg. "The Judge Singlehandedly Trying to Solve the Opioid Crisis." www.bloomberg.com
• Magan, Christopher. "How Opioids Ruined Three Lives." www.twincities.com
• Herzberg, David. "Setting Today's Opioid Epidemic in Historical Context." www.processhistory.org

Chapter 3: What is the Opioid Crisis?, pp. 14–19
• Katz, Josh. "Short Answers to Hard Questions about the Opioid Crisis." www.nytimes.com
• National Institute on Drug Abuse. "Opioid Overdose Crisis." www.drugabuse.gov
• Durden, Tyler. "Drug Overdoses Now the Leading Killer of American Adults Under 50." www.zerohedge.com

• Lopez, German and Sarah Frostenson. "How the opioid epidemic became America's worst drug crisis ever." www.vox.com
• "Opiate Addiction/Opioid Addiction." www.therecoveryvillage.com
• History Channel. "Heroin, Morphine, and Opiates." www.history.com
• "Opiate Withdrawal Timelines, Symptoms, and Treatments." https://americanaddictioncenters.org

Chapter 4: Information Literacy, pp. 20–29
• Collier, Lorna. "Young Victims of the Opioid Crisis." www.apa.org
• Geddes, John. Macleans, "Facing the opioid crisis, an established doctor heads to the streets." www.macleans.ca
• Meridian Treatment Solutions. "Fentanyl Surpasses Heroin in Drug Overdose Death." www.meridiantreatment.com
• Babcock, Pamela. Society for Human Resource Management. "Drugs in Workplace, Understated Crisis." www.shrm.org

Chapter 5: Where Things Stand, pp. 30–39
• Brown, Chris. "How Europe's heroin capital solved its overdose crisis." www.cbc.ca
• Brankovic, Valerie and Sedigh, Hadi. "White House unveils strategy to fight opioid abuse." www.naco.org
• Lopez, German. "One way cities can reduce overdose deaths: open safe spaces for injection heroin." www.vox.com
• Drugs.com "Suboxone." www.drugs.com
• Lupick, Travis. "Portugal drug czar Dr. João Goulão offers advice on the fentanyl crisis ahead of his first visit to Vancouver." www.straight.com
• HAMS Harm Reduction Network. "Seven Countries with Long Term Success in Overcoming a Major Overdose Crisis." http://hams.cc
• Weir, Fred. "Russian answer to opioid epidemic: 'Cold Turkey'." www.csmonitor.com

Chapter 6: Keeping Up to Date, pp. 40–43
• World Affairs Council of Charlotte. "Don't be Left Behind: Knowledge of Current Events is Important!" https://worldaffairscharlotte.wordpress.com
• Hindy, Joe. "10 best news apps for android." www.androidauthority.com
• Summers, Nick. "10 best iPhone apps for keeping on top of the news." https://thenextweb.com

FIND OUT MORE

Finding good source material on the Internet can sometimes be a challenge. When analyzing how reliable the information is, consider these points:

- Who is the author of the page? Is it an expert in the field or a person who experienced the event?

- Is the site well known and up to date? A page that has not been updated for several years probably has out-of-date information.

- Can you verify the facts with another site? Always double-check information.

- Have you checked all possible sites? Don't just look on the first page a search engine provides.

- Remember to try government sites and research papers.

- Have you recorded website addresses and names? Keep this data so you can backtrack later and verify the information you want to use.

WEBSITES

The top 10 U.S. national drug or alcohol-use hotlines:
http://alcohol.addictionblog.org/top-10-national-drug-or-alcohol-use-hotlines

The Canadian Centre on Substance Use and Addiction provides helplines for youth struggling with addiction in all provinces and territories:
www.ccdus.ca/Eng/Pages/Addictions-Treatment-Helplines-Canada.aspx

How to talk to your parents about drugs and alcohol:
www.crchealth.com/troubled-teenagers/teenage-substance-abuse/talking-parents

BOOKS

Carlson, Dale, and Hannah Carlson. *Addiction: The Brain Disease*. Bick Publishing House, 2010.

Heegaard, Marge. *When a Family Is in Trouble: Children Can Cope with Grief from Drug and Alcohol Addiction*. Woodland Press, 1996.

Marcovitz, Hal. *The Opioid Epidemic*. Reference Point Publishing, 2017.

Paris, Stephanie. *Straight Talk: Drugs and Alcohol*. Shell Educational Publishing, 2012.

ABOUT THE AUTHOR

Natalie Hyde has written more than 75 fiction and nonfiction books for kids. She shares her home with a little leopard gecko, and a cat that desperately wants to eat it.

INDEX

addiction, addicts 4, 6, 10, 12, 14, 15, 16, 17, 18, 21, 22, 25, 27, 28–29, 31, 32, 34, 35, 38
age issue 26, 27

bias 8, 9, 11, 21, 40, 41
blogs 11, 31, 42

cannabis 35
chronic pain 6, 35, 38
cocaine 15
codeine 12, 13, 16
cold turkey 38
context 6, 40
current topics 6, 31

death rate 4, 7, 14, 17, 19, 27, 32, 35, 38
debate 5, 6
doctors 9, 12, 13, 15, 16, 17, 18, 20, 21, 24, 26, 32, 38, 41, 42, 43
drug abuse 9, 12, 15, 16, 24, 26, 27, 31, 39
drug companies 6, 9, 11, 13, 18, 20, 21, 37
drug dealers 9, 15, 21
drugs 4, 6, 9, 12, 14, 16, 18, 22, 28, 29, 34, 37

epidemic 5, 21
evidence 9

false information 11, 31, 34–35
fentanyl 12, 13, 17, 33, 35

genes 28
graphics 13

heroin 13, 16, 17, 19, 26, 29, 35, 43
high 16, 24

illegal drugs 15, 16, 32
information literacy 20
Internet 10, 11, 41, 42
interviews 9, 11, 21, 22

key players 9, 12, 22, 39

law enforcement officers 9, 16, 21
laws 15, 21, 32, 33, 41

medical treatment 4, 12
methadone 13, 16, 19, 38
morphine 12, 13, 16, 38
myths 34–35, 41

naloxone 10, 14, 17, 32, 37
narcotics 13
needle exchange 9, 21, 37, 39
neurotransmitters 16
news diet 41, 42

opiates 6, 13, 15, 16, 18
opium 12, 13, 16, 18
overdose 4, 9, 10, 14, 15, 17, 19, 21, 22, 26, 29, 33, 35, 37
oxycodone 12, 16, 18
OcyContin 17, 18

pain management 12, 15, 18, 32
pain relief, painkillers 4, 13, 15, 16, 17, 27, 34, 35

paramedics 9, 10, 15, 19, 21, 33
Percocet 17
perspectives 6, 21, 29
pharmaceutical companies 6, 9, 11, 13, 18, 20, 21, 37
podcasts 11, 42
police 14, 27, 33
poppies 12, 16
prescriptions 16, 18, 27, 32, 34, 35, 37, 43
primary sources 11, 41
Purdue Pharma 18

recreational drugs 16
rehabilitation 25, 29, 37, 39

safe-injection sites 9, 37
secondary sources 11
side effects 6
social media 11
social workers 9, 15
source material 11, 20, 41
street names 15
substance abuse 12, 24

tertiary sources 11
Time and Place Rule 8
trafficking 7, 17

Vicodin 17
vocabulary 12

withdrawal 16, 22
workplace 24, 25